Our Digestion System

Susan Thames

Rourke

Publishing LLC

Vero Beach, Florida 32964

© 2008 Rourke Publishing LLC

www.rourkepublishing.com

PHOTO CREDITS: © David Hernandez: title page; © Renee Brady: pages 7, 15, 21, 22; © Sean Locke: page 4; © Thomas Perkins: page 9; © Justin Horrocks: page 11; © Karen Struthers: page 17; © Don Bayley: page 19; © Brenda McEwan: page 20.

Editor: Robert Stengard-Olliges

Cover design by Michelle Moore.

Library of Congress Cataloging-in-Publication Data

Thames, Susan.
  Our digestion system / Susan Thames.
    p. cm. -- (Our bodies)
  Includes bibliographical references and index.
  ISBN 978-1-60044-510-1 (Hardcover)
  ISBN 978-1-60044-671-9 (Softcover)
  1. Digestion--Juvenile literature. 2. Gastrointestinal system--Juvenile literature. [1. Digestive system.] I. Title.
  QP145.T39 2008
  612.3--dc22
                    2007011806

Printed in the USA

CG/CG

Rourke Publishing

www.rourkepublishing.com – rourke@rourkepublishing.com
Post Office Box 3328, Vero Beach, FL 32964

Table of Contents

Food

Your body needs food
to grow.

What foods do you like?

Wash your hands before you eat.

7

Your Digestion System

Food goes through your body.

You chew food in your mouth.

The chewed food goes down
a tube.

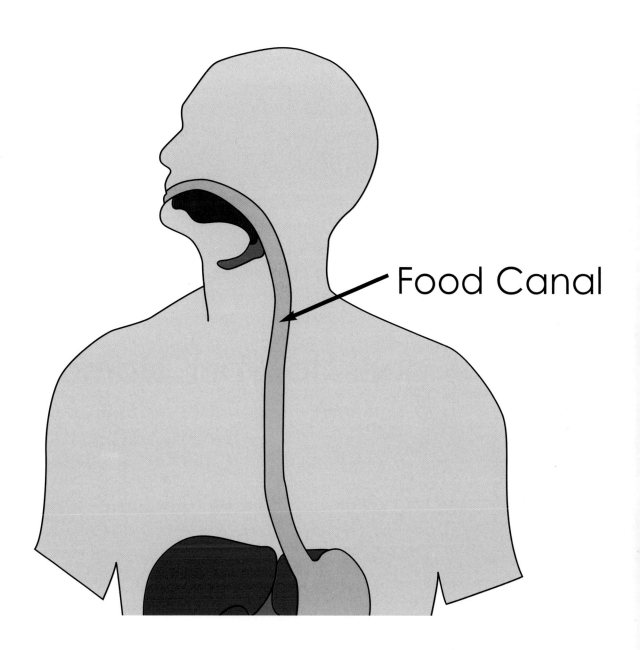

Food Canal

Then it goes to your **stomach**.

Some food stays in your body.

Some food leaves your body.

19

Healthy Body

Your body needs fruits and **grains**.

Your body needs water too.

Food gives you **energy**
to play.

Glossary

energy (EN ur jee) — what makes you move

grains (GRAYNS) — cereal, bread and flour are made from grains

stomach (STUHM uhk) — place where food goes after you eat

Index

Further Reading

Corcoran, Mary. *Quest to Digest*. Charlesbridge Publishing, 2006.

Lindeen, Carol. *My Stomach*. Pebble Books, 2007.

Websites to Visit

www.kidshealth.org

www.healthfinder.gov/kids

www.yucky.discovery.com

About the Author

Susan Thames, a former elementary school teacher, lives in Tampa, Florida. She enjoys spending time with her grandsons and hopes to instill in them a love of reading and a passion for travel.